WEAPONS
AND WARFARE
IN ANCIENT TIMES

The Lerner Archaeology Series

DIGGING UP THE PAST

WEAPONS AND WARFARE IN ANCIENT TIMES

by Rivka Gonen

retold for young readers by Richard L. Currier

 Lerner Publications Company ■ Minneapolis

Designed by Ofra Kamar

LIBRARY OF CONGRESS CATALOGING IN PUBLICATION DATA

Currier, Richard L.
  Weapons and warfare in ancient times.

  (Digging up the Past: The Lerner Archaeology Series)
  SUMMARY: Traces the development of military tactics and
  such items as swords, spears, long-range weapons, artillery,
  and body coverings from prehistory to Roman times.

    1. Arms and armor—Juvenile literature. 2. Military art
  and science—Juvenile literature. [1. Arms and armor] I. Gonen, Rivka, author. II. Title.

  U805.C8 1976   355.8'2   72-10802
  ISBN 0-8225-0832-X

This book is also cataloged under the name of Rivka Gonen.

International Standard Book Number: 0-8225-0832-X
Library of Congress Catalog Card Number: 72-10802

Manufactured in the United States of America

2   3   4   5   6   7   8   9   10   85   84   83   82   81   80   79

CONTENTS

An ancient
Assyrian warrior
armed for battle

I THE STUDY OF ANCIENT WEAPONS

Introduction

In our modern society, the weapons most often used are explosives and firearms, such as pistols, rifles, shotguns, machine guns, grenades, bombs, and missiles. Most of these weapons enable us to attack our enemies even if they are far away. Of course, they enable our enemies to attack us from long distances as well. Modern warfare has reached the point where the soldiers of opposing armies may hardly ever see each other any more. They may detect each others' presence by means of radar, they may aim their guns or missiles with the aid of computers, and they may fire their weapons by simply pushing buttons, never seeing either their enemies or the destruction that their weapons may cause.

This kind of push-button warfare is a great change from the kind of warfare fought in ancient times. In those days, opposing armies were so close together that they could easily shout — or even speak — to each other on the battlefield. Often, in fact, the combatants fought hand-to-hand, pitting their physical strength — and the strength of their weapons — directly against each other in a fight to the death.

Almost all of the weapons used in modern warfare were unknown only a few hundred years ago. For the thousands of years before that, people fought with a great variety of weapons, but none of them were firearms or explosives. This book is about the weapons that people used before the development of industry and modern technology completely changed the nature of weapons and warfare.

In the Beginning

We humans are often said to possess no natural built-in weapons because we lack the long, sharp teeth and claws, the powerful hooves, and the deadly horns and antlers of other animal species. But while our natural

This stone carving from the seventh century B.C. depicts a battle between Assyrian soldiers and desert warriors mounted on camels. Works of art such as this provide valuable information about the weapons used in ancient times.

weapons may not be as impressive as those of a tiger or an elephant, we are not exactly defenseless.

With our open hand, we can inflict a painful, shocking slap. With a closed fist, we can deliver a blow hard enough to stun our enemies or even knock them unconscious. And while our nails and teeth may be no match for those of most other animals our size, they can still cause deep and painful wounds. Even in modern times, these biological "weapons" are commonly used when we humans fight among ourselves, whether we are children fighting on the playground or adults competing at a karate school or in a boxing ring.

Our biological weapons may be suitable for fighting among ourselves, but they are no match for the weapons possessed by many of the large and dangerous animals that human beings have hunted and killed since prehistoric times. To outfight such creatures as bears, wolves, buffaloes, lions, elephants, and walruses, our prehistoric ancestors learned to rely on sticks, stones, and bones. These objects could be shaped into effective weapons and could be carried about, ready for use at any time. From the very beginning, human beings were the only animals that relied on objects they made themselves for the purpose of attacking, capturing, and killing the creatures they hunted for food.

The first humans lived in East Africa two or three million years ago. While they walked erect as we do, their brains were only slightly larger than the brain of the average chimpanzee. In some respects they were more like apes than like human beings, but even these earliest and most primitive of humans made and used weapons. In the beginning, these weapons were probably just stones picked up from the ground and clubs made of tree branches or of animal bones.

Stones are useful as weapons mainly because they can be thrown at the enemy while he is still some distance away. Sticks or clubs are useful because they tend to extend the length of the human arm and thus increase the force of its blows. From the very earliest times, human beings used both of these kinds of weapons. One kind was held in the hand and used for striking blows against a nearby enemy. The other was thrown toward an enemy who was some distance away. As you will see, these two basic types of weapons remained separate and distinct throughout the history of our species.

An Egyptian painting from around 1400 B.C., showing warfare between soldiers riding in chariots

Greek soldiers march into battle carrying long spears and round shields. A vase painting from the 13th century B.C.

For hundreds of thousands of years, humans hunted and attacked, fought and killed with spears, axes, knives, and clubs, some of which were designed for throwing and some for striking or stabbing. Then, only tens of thousands of years ago, people invented something revolutionary: a weapon that could shoot projectiles farther and faster than the human arm could throw them. As far as we know, the first weapons of this type were the bow and arrow and the sling.

Shooting weapons represented an important step in the evolution of humanity, because they marked a clear separation between us and our ape and monkey relatives. An ape can throw a stone or use a tree branch as a club, but no ape or monkey, however brilliant, has the intelligence to make and use a sling or a bow and arrow. After the development of such weapons took place, the original throwing and striking weapons became less important in hunting and warfare, and shooting weapons became more important. By now, almost all the weapons we use in hunting and in warfare are of the shooting variety.

As people developed better and better weapons, they also began to develop ways of protecting them-selves. In this area too, most other animals have a distinct natural advantage over us. Many animals have shells or bony plates to protect them in case of attack. Other animals have thick hides or dense fur coats to shield them from the sharp teeth and claws of their enemies. Still other animals can fly into the air, dive beneath the water, or burrow into the ground when danger threatens. Many species also have a protective camouflage in the color and pattern of their skins, fur, or feathers that allows them to blend into their surroundings so well that they seem to become nearly invisible. We humans have none of these natural defenses, and had to rely on our fleetness of foot and our intelligence to protect us from harm.

Just as people learned to make and use better weapons than those their own bodies could provide, so they also learned to make and use objects to defend themselves against attack. People have used shields, helmets, and body armor since the beginnings of recorded history, and possibly long before that. People also learned long ago to build fortified villages, towns, and cities so that, surrounded by thick, high walls, they could be safe from wild animals and attacking enemy tribes. The study of fortresses and fortified settlements is

This beautiful Greek vase from the sixth century B.C. pictures a struggle between soldiers armed with spears and bows.

A helmet worn by a soldier in the Roman legions

a fascinating part of the history of weapons and warfare, but it is such a large and complicated subject that we would need another entire book to describe it. Thus the defensive measures we will describe here will be only those that the individual carries with him, such as shields, helmets, and body armor.

Where Does Our Information Come From?

Our knowledge of ancient weapons and their use comes from three different kinds of sources. The first is the ancient weapons themselves that have survived to the present day. Over the years, many of these weapons have been preserved — both accidentally and on purpose — in tombs, castles, graves, and ruined cities. Archaeologists — scientists who find and study objects from ancient times — often discover the remains of weapons when they explore an abandoned settlement or the ruins of an ancient city. Many thousands of ancient weapons have found their way into museums and private collections, and they are probably our most important source of information about the weaponry of ancient times.

The problem with most of the ancient weapons we do have is that few of them have survived intact. For the most part, only the metal or stone tips of the weapons lasted, while the wooden shafts or handles and the leather bindings and protective coverings have all decayed and disappeared. Another problem is that since metal was difficult to obtain in ancient times, people almost never deliberately threw away weapons that had become broken and useless. Old axe blades, spearheads, and arrow points were melted down to make new weapons. This meant that few old weapons were discarded in the first place, and of these, fewer still have survived.

One of the most interesting factors affecting the survival of ancient weapons is the different rate at which different metals corrode. Iron

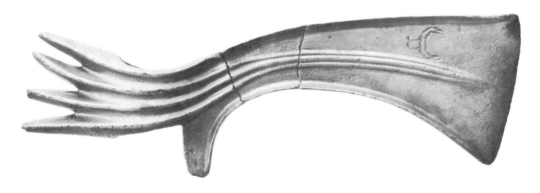

A bronze axe blade found in an ancient temple in Israel. The wooden shaft of the axe has decayed.

This picture of a ruler riding in a war chariot decorated a wall in the palace of the Assyrian king Tiglath-pileser III, who lived in the eighth century B.C.

rusts quite quickly, and iron weapons thus tend to disappear completely after a few hundred years. Copper and bronze, on the other hand, corrode quite slowly, and a tool or weapon made of these metals may survive for thousands of years. This is why we have many more copper and bronze weapons from ancient times than iron weapons, even though the copper and bronze weapons are from much longer ago.

Some of the ancient weapons that survived were found in tombs and temples, where they were often protected from the elements. These weapons, of course, are more easily located than weapons that may have been simply lost on the field of battle in the open countryside. Many of the weapons found in tombs and temples are made of gold and silver, decorated with elaborate designs and inlaid with precious stones. But it is unlikely that weapons of such dazzling beauty were ever used for serious fighting, even by kings and princes (who, in ancient times, marched into battle with their armies).

Weapons such as these were made and used for ceremonial purposes. Some were gifts from one ruler to another, others may have been offerings to ancient gods, while still others were placed in the tombs of rulers when they died, to serve them in the afterlife. While these weapons may not have really been used for fighting, however, they were almost certainly made in the shapes and styles of real fighting weapons of those times. By studying them we can learn much about the real weapons of copper, bronze, and iron, which were far deadlier than any weapon of gold or silver could ever have been.

Ancient works of art are another important source of information about the weapons of ancient societies. Paintings, sculptures, seals, and other objects often depicted ancient rulers and their armies dressed for battle or actually at war. From these pictures we have learned much about what kinds of weapons were made and even how and where they were used. Unfortunately, most of these works of art show only one view or side of the weapon they portray. Some of the large and complex weapons used in ancient warfare cannot be fully understood from a single two-dimensional view. Thus in many cases there is still much about these weapons that remains unknown.

A third important source of information about ancient weapons are

A silver dish showing the Persian king Cyrus II hunting wild animals with a bow and arrow

the ancient writings that have survived. Some ancient documents not only describe the weapons that were used in battle but even explain how they were used. Unfortunately, however, such documents are rare. While the Greeks and Romans were ambitious writers who left behind many old scrolls and manuscripts, many ancient civilizations left few writings behind. And even when these few documents do describe battles and warfare, they rarely describe the weapons that were used.

How Weapons Changed and Developed

Every army wants to obtain and use the best weapons available. Since inferior weapons might well mean defeat and even death in battle, the search for the best possible weapons has always been a matter of life or death for soldiers and military commanders throughout history. Thus it is not surprising that armies have searched hard and well for better weapons and have used every advance in science and technology to build weapons that would be deadlier and more accurate than the weapons in use at that time.

Whenever one group of people have devised a better weapon, however, their enemies have tried, often successfully, to copy these improvements. And when your enemies have the new weapons to use against you, your old means of defense may no longer be good enough. In this way, each new advance in offensive weapons stimulates a new advance in defense, and this stimulates another new advance in offensive weapons again! An example of how this process works can be found in the development of the bow and arrow as a weapon of war. As ancient people found new ways of constructing bows to shoot farther and more powerfully, they also began to develop body armor to protect themselves from the new and improved force of these bows and arrows.

New developments in science and technology have often resulted in the improvement of the accuracy and effectiveness of weapons, both in ancient and in modern times. One of the most important of these developments in ancient times occurred when people learned to use metals. For most of human history, people made sharp points for their spears, axes, knives, and arrows out of stone, bone and wood. But none of these materials could compare with metals like copper and bronze for sharpness and strength. Metal points and blades greatly expanded the number and variety of weapons that could be manufactured. For example, weapons with long, sharp blades (such as swords) simply could not be made out of rock, bone, or wood.

The first metal that ancient people used for weapons was copper, because copper was easily extracted from its ores and worked into the desired shapes. Copper is easily shaped because it is soft, but it is also easily bent or broken for the same reason. After many centuries, people learned to add small amounts of the metal called "tin" to their copper, and this produced the harder and stronger metal called "bronze." Eventually, bronze replaced copper as the most common metal used for making weapons in ancient times.

After about 1000 B.C., people learned how to use iron and how to combine iron with other metals to make it even stronger and more durable. Unlike copper and bronze weapons, which had to be repaired and replaced often, a well-made iron weapon could last a lifetime. These

A wall painting in the tomb of an Egyptian nobleman

changes did not, however, occur quickly. It took hundreds and often even thousands of years for people to learn new ways of using and fashioning metal.

Even when people had the necessary skills, knowledge, and ideas, it still was not always possible to improve the weapons that were actually available. Natural deposits of metal ores were difficult for ancient people to locate. Moreover, mines were often jealously guarded by a few powerful rulers who did not want the source of new and better metals to fall into the hands of their enemies. Means of transportation in the ancient world were slow, and this too hindered the spread of the newer types of metals and weapons.

In some cases, ancient societies were so reluctant to change that they often ignored new resources or technologies, even when these were freely available. Ancient Egypt, for example, while one of the wealthiest, most powerful, and most civilized of all the ancient societies, often lagged far behind its neighbors in the development and use of new weapons. Perhaps this was partly due to the fact that Egypt is protected on all sides by burning deserts that were difficult for its enemies to cross, but it was also due to the great conservatism of the ancient Egyptians. Living in wealth and security in the Nile Valley, where each year the spring floods deposited a rich layer of new soil, and where dams and irrigation ditches assured bountiful crops, the Egyptians became complacent and resisted change of any kind.

In spite of conservatism, poor transportation and communication, scarceness of natural resources, and the jealousy of ancient rulers, however, weapons and warfare changed greatly over the thousands of years from ancient times to the present. Some weapons, such as clubs and spears, were extremely important in the beginning but gradually lost their usefulness and were practically abandoned. Other weapons, such as swords, were unknown to the earliest ancient societies but eventually came to be the ancient soldier's single most important weapon.

In the remainder of this book, we will consider each type of weapon in turn, beginning with the small weapons used in hand-to-hand combat and ending with the mighty machines that could throw huge stones over fortress walls or shoot heavy missiles far across the field of battle. We are sure that you will find this a fascinating and unusual story.

There are three main types of weapons for fighting at close range. The first type is designed to strike a heavy blow that stuns or wounds the victim but does not draw blood. A club is an example of this type of weapon. The second type is also designed for striking, but this weapon will inflict a deep gash. Sabres and battle axes are weapons of this type. The third type of close-range weapon is designed for stabbing or piercing. Examples of piercing weapons are daggers, spears, and the long, thin swords used for dueling by Hollywood heroes and villians.

As each of these three types of weapons was developed in turn, people tended to rely more upon the new weapon and less upon the type that preceeded it. When the ancient metal workers began producing sharp and deadly battle axes, for example, warriors used them in preference to the simple club. Similarly, when metal-working technology advanced to the point where long, thin metal blades could be made for spears and swords, these stabbing weapons rapidly replaced the axe as the most popular instrument of battle.

The Mace

The club is undoubtedly one of the oldest of all weapons. Prehistoric people probably used many different types of clubs, but because these weapons were made of wood they have not survived. Since that time, however, tribal people all over the world have made and used wooden clubs; in those societies clubs have played important roles both in ceremonial life and in war.

Ancient clubs were made so that the business end was thicker and heavier than the grasping end, but there was a limit to how thick a wooden club could be at one end while remaining effective as a fighting weapon. So the people of the ancient Middle East began to experiment with ways of making the end of the club heavier by using other, denser materials. When special weights were fastened to the end of a war club, the weapon that we call the "mace" came into being.

The mace was made of two parts: a wooden handle and a stone or metal weight attached to one end of the handle. These weights were made in the shape of doughnuts — round circles with holes in the centers. The wooden shaft was inserted into the holes, and the end of the shaft was secured so that the weights would not fly off when a warrior swung the mace at his enemy. Some of these ancient mace heads were even ornamented with designs carved into the surface of the stone or metal.

Some ancient societies preferred the mace more than others. The Egyptians and their neighbors considered the mace one of their most important weapons, and they used it with great skill against their enemies. But the Mesopotamians, who lived farther to the east, did not rely on the mace. Mesopotamian soldiers wore helmets in battle at a very early period of ancient history, and these helmets protected them so well against blows from clubs and maces that the armies of that region soon abandoned the mace. Instead, they began to use spears and axes, which could pierce helmets and inflict wounds that the mace could not produce.

Not surprisingly, the ancient Egyptians continued to use the mace until long after other ancient people had abandoned it. At one point, the Egyptians tried to improve the mace by shaping its weighted head into the form of a disc with a somewhat sharpened edge. While this gave the Egyptian mace a slight cutting action, it was not enough to prove effective against the helmets and armor of enemy soldiers, and finally even the conservative Egyptians abandoned the mace forever.

Curiously, the mace was revived almost 4,000 years later, during the Middle Ages in Europe and Asia. At that time, close-range combat between heavily armored warriors was common. To suit the needs of a new kind of warfare, the mace was made in a very new and wicked shape: a cluster of spikes projected from the weighted end of the club. These spikes were designed to pierce the metal armor of the period and inflict deep wounds.

While it has seldom been used as a serious weapon for nearly 5,000 years, the mace has nevertheless retained its ancient significance as a symbol of authority. In the paintings of the ancient Egyptians, the mace

Above: The Egyptian king Narmer prepares to dispatch an enemy with a blow from his mace.

Left: A collection of ancient bronze mace heads found in Israel

The Egyptian god Horus holding a mace as a symbol of victory

appears in the hands of kings and gods as the symbol of victory on the battlefield. Ever since that time, the mace has been a symbol of power and authority. This symbol persists even in modern times as the scepters of kings and the batons of field marshals, both of which are simply modern representations of this most ancient of weapons.

The Battle Axe

The mace gradually fell into disuse on the battlefield because it was unable to pierce through the helmets and armor worn by the opposing armies. The battle axe, however, already in use as a deadly cutting and slashing weapon, could be modified to pierce through helmets and protective armor. Thus it gradually took over the job that the mace had done. In fact, you might visualize the axe

as basically a club to which a cutting or piercing blade has been attached. In time, two different types of battle axe appeared. One had a broad, curved blade, and it was designed to attack the unprotected body. The other type had a long, pointed blade, and it was designed mainly to pierce through an enemy's helmet and body armor.

One of the most difficult problems faced by the ancient weapon smiths was that of joining a weapon's metal blade to its wooden shaft or handle. The process of attaching the blade to the shaft is called "hafting," and two different methods of hafting were common in ancient times. The first method was to make the blade with a long strip of metal attached to it. This strip is called a "tang." (You can see an example of a tang on an ordinary carpenter's file, which usually has a tang an inch or two long at one end.) The tang on a blade is made to be inserted into a hole drilled in the shaft or handle. When this is done, the tang is secured to the handle with rivets or other binding materials. An ordinary kitchen knife is hafted in this way.

The other method of hafting was accomplished by means of a device called a "socket." A socket is a tube, in this case made of metal, attached

Thutmose IV, ruler of Egypt, wielding a tanged battle axe with a narrow blade

to the end of the blade that was to be joined to the wooden shaft. The shaft was simply inserted into the socket and held there by rivets that passed through holes in both the socket and the shaft. If you would like to see an example of socket hafting, take a close look at a common garden shovel.

Each of these two methods of hafting has its own particular advantage. The main advantage of the socket is its great strength, which is why it is used for objects like garden shovels, which must bear tremendous stress. Because socket hafting is so strong, ancient weapon smiths used it for battle axes that were designed to pierce armor. No doubt the heavy blows that the axe would have to withstand as a warrior tried to pierce through his enemy's armor required the strongest kind of hafting available.

The tang, on the other hand, has certain advantages over the socket. It is far quicker, easier, and cheaper to make. In addition, it is lighter, because far less metal is required to make a narrow, pointed tang than to make a long, tubular socket. Perhaps it was for these reasons that the broad-bladed cutting axe, which did not have to withstand the terrible blows of the armor-piercing axe, was

hafted by means of the tang.

Although the tanged cutting axe came first, the socketed piercing axe was not long in appearing. By 2500 B.C., the civilizations of Mesopotamia — in what is now modern Iraq — had developed socketed axes, probably to cope with the helmets and armor that had come into use in that part of the ancient world. As usual, the Egyptians lagged behind. Since the Egyptians and their neighbors never used much armor, they had less need for a socketed piercing axe. In later times, when the Egyptians did face armies that wore armor for protection, they simply made their tanged axes narrower, enabling them to be used for piercing.

In time, the piercing axe became more and more important, while the cutting axe became less important. One reason for this was the increased use of helmets and body armor by the armies of the ancient world, but an equally important reason was the development of the sword. The sword proved to be a better cutting and slashing weapon than the battle axe, and the mightiest armies of ancient times soon came to rely on this deadly new weapon. In fact, the ancient Romans — who had the largest and most successful army of the ancient world — never used the

An Egyptian soldier attacks an unarmed enemy with a broad-bladed cutting axe.

battle axe at all. The less civilized tribes of northern Europe and Asia, however, did continue to make and use battle axes even after the Roman Empire collapsed and its great army disappeared.

The battle axe was one of the most versatile and useful weapons of ancient times. In addition to the standard cutting and piercing axes, there were huge battle axes so heavy that a warrior had to use both hands to wield them. On the other hand, there were axes made so small and light that they were mainly designed for throwing, and they were especially balanced for this purpose. Such axes, in fact, are not really close-range weapons at all. To be precise, we would have to classify them as medium-range missiles!

Like the mace, the battle axe remained important for ceremonial purposes long after it ceased to be a useful weapon on the battlefield. The broad-blade Danish battle axe was the symbol of the English royal court during the Middle Ages. In an earlier period, the Romans used as a symbol of their rule an axe with a bundle of rods bound together around the handle. This purely symbolic weapon was carried in Imperial ceremonies and processions before the highest officials of the Roman Empire. The Roman ceremonial axe was called the *fasces* (pronounced FASH-eez), and it was adopted by a political movement that came to power in part of Europe during the 1930s. These people called themselves "fascists," and they used the *fasces* as a symbol of their power.

The Development of the Sword

Hand-to-hand combat in ancient times is often pictured as a duel between two skillful and daring swordsmen, but, in the early period of ancient history, swords did not even exist. The sword came into use less than 3,000 years ago, long after the mace, the battle axe, the bow and arrow, the helmet and armor, and the spear had become standard equipment for the ancient soldier. Our image of the dashing swordsman who rescued fair maidens in distress comes not from ancient times at all but rather from the Middle Ages in Europe, long after the ancient civilizations of Greece, Rome, Mesopotamia, and Egypt had disappeared.

There were two reasons why the arsenal of the early warriors did not include the sword. The first reason was that the earliest metals available in ancient times were too soft and weak to be used for making swords. A long, thin blade of even the hardest copper or bronze would never be strong enough to withstand the strain of battle. Thus there were limits to the length and thinness of the weapons that could be made of these metals. If these limits were passed, the weapons would bend or break.

The second reason is that the early metal smiths simply did not know how to forge a metal object into a large, long shape. Most ancient weapons consisted of a long shaft or handle to which a fairly small blade was attached, whereas a sword is nearly all blade. Only the hilt, a short handle by which the sword is meant to be grasped, is made of wood or bone.

The ancestor of the modern sword was the ancient bronze dagger. The blade of this weapon was less than 12 inches (30 centimeters) in length, and it was riveted to a wooden or bone handle. The dagger was a popular weapon in the ancient world until about 1500 B.C., and numerous examples have been found in the excavations of ancient ruins. Some of the most beautiful daggers of ancient times have been found in the royal tombs of the ancient Mesopotamians. Several of these were made of solid gold, with hilts of ivory or rare stone and finely wrought sheaths of gold.

When the smiths began to forge daggers in one piece, with blade and hilt together as a single unit, they created a weapon that no longer had the old problem of joining the blade to the handle. Even more important, the development of iron working had finally given ancient craftsmen a material hard and strong enough to be fashioned into a long, thin blade. At last, the technical problems that had stood in the way of the development of the sword had been solved.

The Rapier and the Sabre

While the short-bladed dagger was useful mainly for stabbing, a weapon with a much longer blade could be used either for stabbing or for striking. These two different ways of attacking led to the development of two basically different types of swords. One, called the "rapier," was designed for stabbing with a thrusting motion. The rapier is long, thin, and light in weight, with a sharp point for piercing. The heavy part of the weapon is placed near the hilt, so that the swordsman can hold the tip of the weapon high and ma-

neuver it around quickly during a sword fight.

The other type of sword, called the "sabre," was designed for slashing with a striking motion. The sabre has a thick, heavy blade, with a sharp cutting edge, and it is heaviest not at the hilt but down near the tip of the blade, adding extra weight to the force of the blow. In contrast to the straight blade of the rapier, the blade of the sabre is often curved, because this shape tends to inflict a particularly long wound. Rapiers were made in one basic shape: long, straight, and narrow. Sabres, on the other hand, were made in a variety of shapes. They were made both curved and straight, both long and short, and both with one cutting edge and with two.

At different periods in ancient

This Egyptian wall relief from the 13th century B.C. shows a group of Libyan soldiers armed with very long rapiers.

history, these two different types of swords rose and fell in popularity. Ancient armies needed both stabbing and striking weapons, and a sword of either the sabre or the rapier type was used for one of these two purposes. If the army used battle axes as striking weapons, they tended to favor a rapier type of sword. On the other hand, some armies used spears as stabbing weapons, and therefore they favored a sword with striking power.

Dual-Purpose Swords

One of the most useful and important swords of ancient times was first produced in eastern Europe, in the region that is now the nation of Hungary. This was a straight, two-edged sword, heavy enough to be used as a sabre but sufficiently long and pointed at the end to be used as a thrusting weapon as well. This dual-purpose sword was adopted by the Greeks, who carried it to other lands of the ancient world on their missions of trade and colonization.

Above: In this battle scene, soldiers using long straight swords fight alongside of other soldiers wielding curved sabres

Right: Socketed bronze axe heads made by the ancient inhabitants of Iran

Overleaf left and right: The Sumerian army in battle array, depicted on the Standard of Ur, a 4,500-year-old wooden panel inlaid with shell and lapis lazuli

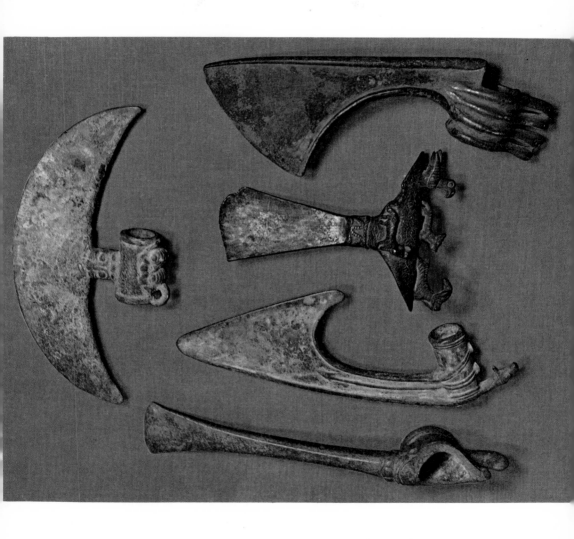

Although this early dual-purpose sword disappeared after 1000 B.C., a sword of similar but more efficient design was adopted by the Romans many hundreds of years later. This was the famous *gladius,* or "Spanish sword" (so called because it was made of iron from Spain), the standard sword of the mighty Roman legions. The *gladius* was about two feet (60 centimeters) long, with a straight, two-edged blade that tapered to a sharp point at the end. Although it was light in weight, the *gladius* had such a perfect balance that it was deadly when used as a sabre. With a single downward stroke, the Roman soldier could use it to split open the armor of his adversary. Yet the *gladius'* light weight and straight, pointed shape made it an effective thrusting weapon as well.

You have probably heard of the famous sword fighters of Roman times called "gladiators." These slaves, war captives, and other prisoners, armed with the *gladius,* were pitted against wild animals — or against each other — in battles to the death. These battles were considered great sport in ancient Rome, and thousands flocked to the great public arenas to watch them.

Left: Two daggers with golden sheaths, found in the tomb of the Egyptian pharoah Tutankhamon

The Curved Sabre of the East

While the nations of the West developed many fine straight swords, the peoples of the East specialized in the development of the curved sabre, perhaps the most deadly close-range weapon of ancient times. The ancestor of the curved sabre was a weapon called the "sickle-sword," which enjoyed great popularity among the armies of the ancient Middle East from 2000 to 1000 B.C.

A sickle is a crescent-shaped blade set on a wooden handle, and it is used in many peasant societies for harvesting grain. The sharp cutting edge of the sickle is on the inside of the curve, so that the blade can be hooked around a bunch of grain to cut it.

The sickle-sword, however, was sharpened on the outside of the curve, and the blade was set on the end of a long handle, so that it curved back from the end of the shaft. The sickle-sword was a striking weapon, wielded with a swinging motion almost like a whip.

At first, the handle of the sickle-sword was twice as long as the blade, but in time the blade gradually became longer and heavier and the handle became shorter. In the end, the sickle-sword evolved into a type of curved sabre that the armies of

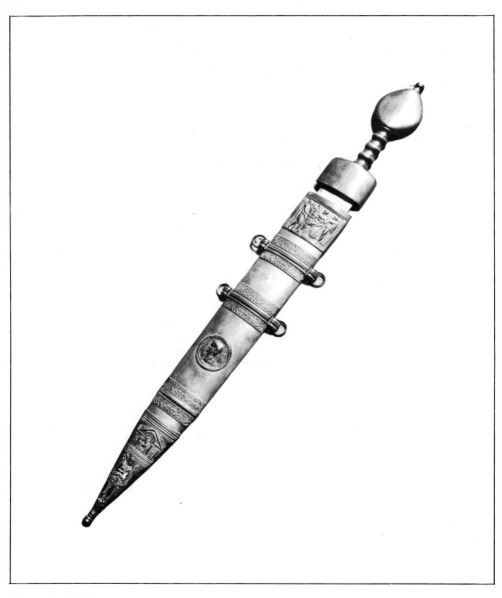

The sheathed *gladius* of the Roman emperor Tiberius. The hilt is reconstructed.

This relief carved on a stone coffin shows Roman soldiers using the *gladius*.

the East used with deadly effectiveness. For example, the Greeks of classical times, who used spears as stabbing weapons, used a curved sabre called the *kopis* as a striking weapon. Paintings on many ancient Greek vases show Greek warriors with the *kopis* raised above their

Ramses III, Pharoah of Egypt, threatens a trembling enemy soldier with a short-handled sickle-sword.

heads, ready to deliver a staggering blow. These curved sabres were made and used in the East until modern times, and they have been a favorite weapon of horsemen from the Russian steppes to the deserts of Arabia.

In this chapter, we have been able to give you only a very brief summary of some of the most important and interesting close-range weapons. While clubs and maces were used to only a limited extent in the ancient world, the number and variety of battle axes, knives, daggers, and swords was enormous. Even so, the ancient warrior was not always forced to engage in hand-to-hand combat. If he were lucky, he might defeat his enemies while they were still some distance away. This he could do with the medium-range weapons of ancient warfare, the subjects of our next chapter.

III SPEARS AND JAVELINS

Spears and javelins are quite similar in appearance; they are both long wooden shafts to which sharp metal points or blades have been attached. Both weapons are used for combat at medium range — that is at distances from a few feet (one to two meters) to several yards (5 to 15 meters). These weapons thus fall between the close-range weapons of hand-to-hand combat and such long-range weapons as arrows, crossbows, and catapults.

The basic difference between a spear and a javelin is that a spear is made to be held in the hands and used for stabbing while the javelin is meant to be thrown. There is, however, no sharp distinction between these two weapons, and in emergencies the spear can be thrown like a javelin, while the javelin can be used for stabbing, like a spear. Sometimes, in fact, archaeologists are not entirely sure whether a particular metal point that they find originally belonged to a spear or a javelin. There were undoubtedly weapons made in ancient times that could be used for either purpose.

In general, however, the spear and the javelin are constructed differently, each for its own special purpose. The spear is heavier, with its weight concentrated near the tip of the blade. The javelin, on the other hand, tends to be lighter, with the weight toward the middle, for better balance.

These long, pointed shafts are among the oldest and most basic weapons of all, and their ancestor is a simple pointed stick. A long, straight shaft of wood, sharpened to a point (and with the point hardened by fire), has been a basic human weapon since prehistoric times. Nearly all known tribal people, whatever their level of technological achievement, have used pointed sticks of this type for hunting, for fighting, and for digging up roots and other wild foods. Even in the ancient world, pointed sticks with fire-hardened tips were used in warfare; the

The royal guard of the Persian king Darius I armed with long spears and bows

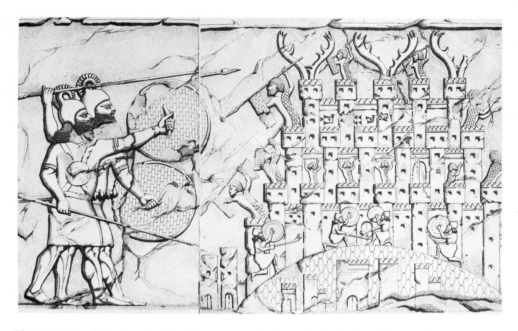

The spearmen of the Assyrian king Sargon approach the walls of a besieged city that has been set on fire.

Romans wrote of encounters with German tribes who used such weapons. As a matter of fact, the Greek word for spear means "tree" or "stem."

Spearmen of the Ancient Armies

For a long time, the spear was the ancient soldier's principal weapon, in much the same way that the rifle is the principal weapon of the modern soldier. Toward the end of ancient times, when metal working became sufficiently advanced, the sword

took over as the principal weapon of ancient warfare, but, until then, the spear reigned supreme. Even when the first bronze daggers and the earliest iron swords were being made, the spear continued to be the favorite weapon of ancient armies, for it had certain advantages over the sword.

For one thing, the spear was cheaper and easier to produce. Spearheads required far less metal than swords, and they were smaller and simpler in design. Yet the spear's heavy wooden shaft gave it tremen-

Hunters armed with spears, bows, and maces appear on this fragment of an ancient paint palette from Egypt.

dous striking power; a well-made spear could pierce through almost any type of shield or armor. Finally, the spears of ancient times were quite long — considerably longer than a man is tall — and thus they could be used to attack an opponent from a distance of several feet. For a long time, close-range weapons such as daggers or swords were used only as a last resort, if a soldier had been unable to wound or kill his opponent by using a spear.

The spear appears on the earliest ancient monument, for instance, in a series of famous hunting scenes left behind by the Egyptians of 3000 B.C. A carved monument from Mesopotamia, also from 3000 B.C., shows a hunter who has stabbed a lion with his long spear. Lion hunting was considered a noble and courageous sport in the ancient Middle East, and the ancient Greeks seem to have engaged in lion hunting as well. A dagger found in a Greek tomb from the Bronze Age bears a design showing lion hunters with spears. If the ancient artist did not exaggerate the length of the spears in this drawing, these hunters were using spears more than 15 feet (four and a half meters) long!

The ancient Greeks developed the use of the spear in warfare to a high degree, using a special formation of spearmen called a *phalanx* to attack the enemy on the battlefield. The spearmen would line up together, forming a solid row, with their shields in front of them and their spears thrust outward. They formed a kind of living wall from which a forest of spears projected. At the

A portion of a Bronze-Age dagger from Greece showing lion hunters with extremely long spears

signal to attack, the *phalanx* began to run across the battlefield, advancing straight toward the enemy troops.

The key to the success of the *phalanx* was not only in the courage of the spearmen but also in their discipline and mutual trust. The safety of each member depended on the other members of the *phalanx*. If all kept their places during an attack, all would be safe, but if any soldier broke ranks and ran, a gap would be left in the *phalanx* that would make it vulnerable to attack. A well-trained and disciplined group of spearmen, attacking in the *phalanx* formation, was nearly impossible to stop.

The ancient Greeks had a high regard for the spear, and they considered it their most important weapon for more than a thousand years, beginning in the Bronze Age and continuing through the time of Alexander the Great. Alexander carved out an immense empire in the Middle East about 300 years before the birth of Christ, and the spears used by his conquering army were truly immense. These enormous spears were about 23 feet (seven meters) long — the length of an average-sized living room. The *phalanx* in Alexander's army was formed of several rows of spearmen, one behind the other. Their spears were so long that the tips of the spears held by the soldiers in the fourth and fifth rows back would project out in front of the soldiers in the first row!

The Romans adopted this method of warfare along with much else that they learned from the Greeks, but they enjoyed less success with it than the Greeks had before them. When a group of uncivilized tribes from northwestern Europe invaded the

Above: A *phalanx* of Greek soldiers moves into battle to the accompaniment of a rousing tune played by a young flutist.
Overleaf: A mosaic floor from Pompeii depicting a decisive battle between Alexander the Great (left) and the Persian king Darius (right). The long spears carried by Alexander's soldiers can be clearly seen in the background.

territory near Rome in 370 B.C., the Romans discovered that their heavy spears and unwieldy *phalanx* formations were unsuited to the hilly terrain of their Italian homeland — and also unsuited to warfare with the lightly armed and highly mobile tribesmen. Therefore the Romans reorganized their army, making it quicker and more flexible, and they began to rely more on the sword than on the spear as their main offensive weapon. Even so, the greatest shame a Roman soldier could experience was to lose his spear in battle, and a shorter, broad-bladed spear continued to be an important part of the Roman army's arsenal of weapons.

The Javelin

Although the javelin was never considered the most important weapon in any ancient army, and although it was generally less important than the spear, this interesting weapon could do things no other weapon was capable of. No bow, for example, could shoot an arrow even half as heavy as a javelin. The javelin could thus penetrate in situations where an arrow would simply glance off harmlessly. Spears and battle axes were neither of the correct weight nor correctly balanced for

throwing, and they could not be thrown either as far or as accurately as the javelin. Between the spear and the arrow, therefore, the javelin filled a significant gap.

Javelin throwers were specially trained soldiers, and they often fought alongside the slinger and archers, warriors who specialized in handling long-range missiles. Each javelin thrower carried several javelins, so that he could throw them whenever and wherever he saw an opportunity. Javelins were also carried on chariots (small, light wagons used in ancient warfare), in a tube-shaped container called a "quiver." Later, when soldiers mounted on horseback became a standard part of all organized armies, the javelin found yet another important place as a part of the mounted soldier's regular equipment.

One of the interesting facts about the history of the javelin concerns its relationship to the bow and arrow. During periods of history when the bow and arrow was seldom used in warfare, the javelin was particularly important. But when the bow was improved and made to shoot heavier arrows with greater force, the javelin declined in importance.

Perhaps the best known javelin of ancient times was that used by the

Roman soldiers. Although the Roman armies had groups of archers, the ordinary Roman soldier, armed with his sword (the famous *gladius*) and shield, did not carry a bow. Thus the javelin was the only weapon that he could use as a missile, to strike his opponent while he was still some distance away. This Roman javelin had a long, narrow head, a long socket, and a wooden shaft of medium length. The blade was about two and a half feet (75 centimeters) long, the socket was the same length, and the shaft was about five feet (one and a half meters) long. At the very tip of this long blade there was another, much smaller blade, about four inches (10 centimeters) long, attached by a short bar of soft iron. When this javelin struck its victim, the soft iron bar would bend, causing the small blade to become twisted sideways in the wound and making the

javelin almost impossible to pull out. If the Roman soldier could successfully harpoon his opponent with this deadly weapon, he could make short work of him with his sword.

The javelin had the greatest range and the greatest striking power of any missile that was thrown with the hand. But of course there are limits to the speed and force with which the human hand and arm can throw an object over a long distance. Shooting weapons, however, are simple machines that can concentrate the power of the human body and suddenly release it, propelling a missile farther and faster than the hand and arm alone can do. In the next chapter, we will look at some of the shooting weapons that the ancient soldier carried with him — weapons that gradually grew more powerful, more complex, and more important in the warfare of ancient times.

IV LONG-RANGE WEAPONS

The great advantage of long-range weapons is that they can be used to attack an opponent while he is still far away. If the soldiers on both sides have long-range weapons, they may be more or less evenly matched. But if only one of the soldiers has such a weapon, he has a great advantage, because he can attack the other, running to keep away from close-range weapons and continuing to inflict damage.

This principle is well illustrated by the biblical story of the battle between David, the Hebrew shepherd boy, and Goliath, the Philistine warrior. According to the Bible, Goliath went into battle wearing a brass helmet, a coat of mail (a type of armor made of many small metal links fastened together), and brass armor on his legs. He was armed with a spear and another weapon, either a javelin or a sword, and a shield bearer held a shield in front of him. Against this collection of weapons and equipment, David had only a simple sling, which he used to bombard his opponent with stones hurled at high speed. Goliath was struck in the head with one of these stones and knocked unconscious before he could ever get close enough to David to attack with his medium- and close-range weapons.

Since the main advantage of the long-range weapon is not in the force of its blow but in the distance it can travel, it is not surprising that much of the development of long-range weapons in ancient times resulted from a continual search for weapons that had a greater and greater range.

The Sling

The sling is one of the simplest and most inexpensive weapons ever invented, and it has been used since the earliest times, especially by poor farmers and shepherds. In fact, the long, heavy staff of the shepherd, combined with the sling, is an effective combination of short- and long-range weapons. Used with skill, these weapons can challenge even an armored soldier equipped with sword and spear.

The slingshot we are familiar with is a forked stick, with a pair of heavy rubber bands attached at one end to the stick and at the other end to a leather pouch in which the missiles are placed. The sling of ancient times, however, is much simpler. It consists of nothing more than a leather pouch to which two long leather thongs are attached. This is the type of sling that David used to defeat Goliath. While much practice is necessary before it can be used with skill, it is a far more powerful weapon than the forked-stick and rubber-band variety of sling.

To shoot a stone with this type of sling, the slinger places the stone in the leather pouch and whirls the sling around and around over his head. The faster the sling whirls, the greater speed and force the stone will have when it is finally released. The slinger then released one of the thongs, causing the pouch to open and the stone to fly out. Needless to say, it requires great skill to know exactly when to let go of the thong so as to shoot the stone in the desired direction.

Since leather decays and deteriorates quite rapidly, and since sling

An Egyptian slinger from about 1900 B.C.

stones look just like any other round stones, it is not surprising that no examples of ancient slings have ever been found. A picture of soldiers using the sling in warfare has been found in an Egyptian tomb dating from around 2000 B.C., however, and a sculptured wall in Mesopotamia from about 1000 B.C. also shows soldiers using the sling. From these and other records that have survived, it is clear that the sling was especially useful when an army was attacking a fortress or a fortified city. The sling was one of the few weapons capable of shooting a missile high enough to sail over the top of a city's defenses and land inside the city walls.

The Greeks, who never tired of using their imagination and technical skill to improve the weapons of ancient times, hired slingers from the islands of Crete and Rhodes to fight with the armies from the city-states of the Greek mainland. Eventually, the Greeks hit upon the idea of making sling stones out of lead, instead of relying upon pebbles picked up from the ground. Because the lead missiles were so much heavier than the stone ones, they could be thrown much farther. In fact, one Greek general wrote that the lead missiles gave the sling twice its former range — greater, in many cases, than the range of the bow and arrow.

In the ruins of one Greek city, which had surrendered to a besieging army in 348 B.C., archaeologists found sling stones of lead that had been shot into the city by the attacking army. Some of the missiles are inscribed with the name of the ruler of those attacking forces, while others bear the names of some of the commanders. Still other stones were inscribed with taunting messages, such as one that says, "A nasty gift."

The Development
of the Bow and Arrow

While the sling was used effectively by ancient armies from time to

time, it was never considered a basic and indispensable shooting weapon. The bow and arrow, on the other hand, was the main long-range weapon of ancient armies from the time it was first used in warfare until the invention of firearms a few hundred years ago.

Throughout ancient history, people were constantly seeking ways to improve the effectiveness of the bow and arrow, mainly by trying to increase its range. This was for a good reason. If your own archers have greater range than the enemy's archers, then you can attack your enemy while he is still powerless to attack you. Thus the army that has the greatest range in archery has a definite advantage on the battlefield. Because it was such a decisive weapon in ancient warfare, the bow and arrow often affected the outcome of a battle and, in some cases, even an entire war.

For a while, the physical limitations of the human body — and the nature of the materials the bow was made of — seemed to stand in the way of any significant improvement in the range and striking power of the bow and arrow. First, there was the problem of how to pull the bowstring back as far as possible before releasing the arrow. Using the right

Left: Assyrian slingers (bottom) approach the walls of a besieged city.

hand, it is physically impossible to pull a tight bowstring back past the right ear.

Then there was the problem of finding materials of sufficient flexibility and strength to make the bow with. If the bow is too flexible, it will lack power, but if it is too stiff, it will break when it is repeatedly bent to the maximum extent. Finally, even a strong yet flexible bow must not be too hard to draw, or else the archer will not be able to use it. Thus the power of the bow is partly limited by the strength of the archer's arm.

Arrows

Arrows were made in a variety of shapes and sizes to serve a variety of different purposes. A heavy arrow strikes with sufficient force to penetrate armor. A light arrow, on the other hand, has a far greater range, but it does not strike with much force.

The point of the arrow, called the "arrowhead," has always been made of a hard material that can be shaped and given a sharp cutting edge. During prehistoric times, arrowheads were made of bone or carefully chipped stone, but in ancient times they were made first of copper, then of bronze, and finally of iron. With few

exceptions, arrowheads have always been either triangular or leaf-shaped, ending in a sharp point. Metal arrowheads were usually made with tangs for hafting, but one group of ancient archers used arrowheads shaped like long, thin pyramids joined to the shaft of the arrow by means of small sockets.

In comparison with spears and javelins, arrows were usually not very long, about half the length of the bow itself. One of the more difficult tasks involved in making arrows was producing a shaft that was perfectly straight. Even a slight bend or twist in the shaft would prevent the arrow from flying straight and true. Likely as not, a bent or twisted arrow would fail to hit its mark. The feathers that were glued to the other end of the arrow were often set at a slight angle so that the arrow would spin in flight. This tended to insure that the path of the arrow would be straight. The ancient Persians, who were among the best archers of ancient times, called these feathers "messengers of death."

Bows, Simple and Complex

A single piece of solid wood, properly aged and carved into shape, is the bow of prehistoric times. This kind of bow is still used by many

hunting and gathering tribes living in remote forests and jungles today. It is called the "simple bow" because it is constructed of basically only two parts: a wooden bow and a bowstring. Since a piece of wood will not bend very far before it breaks, the simple bow has to be made very long so that the string can be pulled back a fair distance without forcing the wooden bow into a sharp curve. The simple bows of some hunting tribes are nearly as long as the hunters themselves are tall!

A picture of a hunter using the simple bow appears on a monument from Mesopotamia dating from around 3000 B.C. Not long after that time, however, the more civilized people of the ancient world, such as the Mesopotamians and the Egyptians, began to develop more complex bows. The simple bow nevertheless continued in use among many of the less advanced people of the ancient world, especially in western and northern Europe, where it survived until the 16th century A.D.

A somewhat improved form of the bow is the "reinforced bow," which is made with strips of wood or sinew glued to the back (the part of the bow that faces forward when the archer is ready to shoot). These reinforcements enabled the bow to be bent much further without breaking. The reinforced bow was especially important in regions where it was difficult to obtain the proper kind of wood for making bows. The Eskimos, who had no trees at all in their natural environment, made bows out of carved pieces of bone that they lashed together and reinforced with sinew to prevent them from breaking when the bowstring was drawn.

The most advanced type of bow is called the "composite bow." It is made of several different types of materials glued together to make a strong, flexible bow that can be bent into a deep curve and not lose its strength and that releases the arrow in a smooth, even burst of power. The finest of these bows can shoot a light arrow a distance of more than a third of a mile (550 meters)!

The composite bow first appeared around 2500 B.C. in Mesopotamia, and it was soon adopted by the greatest armies of early ancient times, who considered it their most important weapon. In recent times, the finest composite bows were made by Turkish bow makers, who made bows from five pieces of wood (of three different varieties), a layer of horn, and a layer of sinew. Each material was shaped and treated in special ways to give its own special

Left: A hunter using a heavy simple bow is pictured on this ancient monument from Mesopotamia.

Above: Egyptian archers with simple bows

Left: This monument from Mesopotamia shows
the powerful ruler Naram-Sin carrying a composite bow and trampling on the bodies of his
fallen enemies.

characteristic to the final product. This is a far cry from a simple curved piece of wood!

This concludes our description of the most common and most important weapons that the soldiers of ancient times carried with them. Ancient armies did use other weapons, but most of them were complex machines far too large to carry.

Before we turn our attention to those huge and curious machines, however, we thought you might like to know about some of the special equipment the ancient soldier used to protect himself on the field of battle.

The Scythian archer painted on this Greek plate is shown holding the most advanced kind of composite bow made in ancient times.

V SHIELDS, HELMETS, AND BODY ARMOR

From the earliest periods of ancient history, people have tried to devise ways of protecting the warrior from the harm that his enemies wished to inflict upon him. Ideally, the warrior would have been armored from head to toe and would have carried a shield around with him for good measure. In that way, his entire body would have been protected from harm. But in reality, a warrior dressed in armor from head to foot is almost incapable of fighting his enemies. Most of his strength and energy is spent simply carrying the heavy armor around. And with one hand occupied in carrying a shield, the poor soldier would be able to do little besides wave his free arm about.

On the other hand, a soldier who was completely unprotected from the swords, axes, slings, and arrows of his opponents might not last very long on the battlefield. Thus, in actual practice, a compromise was reached. The soldier would wear armor, but he would wear it only over those parts of his body that were most vital or most vulnerable to attack, such as the head and the chest. He would carry a shield, but it would not be of enormous size, so that the task of carrying and supporting the shield did not completely immobilize his entire arm.

The crew of an Assyrian battle chariot. The two soldiers in the back of the chariot are holding small shields to protect themselves and their companions from enemy arrows.

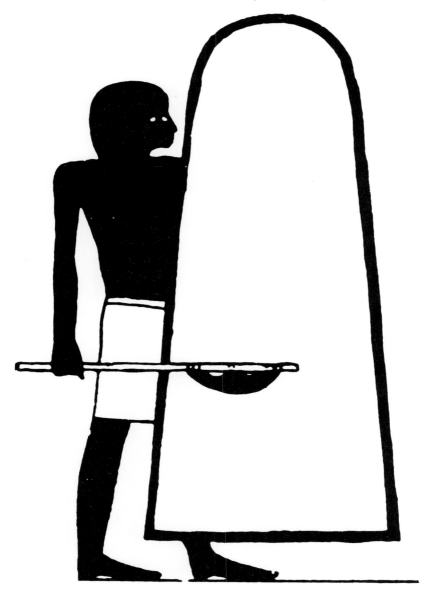

An Egyptian soldier of the 20th century B.C. armed with a broad cutting axe and a large shield

This conflict between the need for protection and the need for lightness and freedom of movement on the battlefield resulted in a constant effort to find just the right balance between these two basic requirements. Whenever a new weapon was developed, however, the need for defensive equipment changed. The appearance of the mace, for example, led to the development of the helmet, and the use of the helmet finally led to the disappearance of the mace, because it did not prove effective against helmeted troops.

The Shield

The shield is an obstacle that the warrior tries to place between himself and his enemy. Its usefulness is due to the fact that it can be moved into position to protect almost any part of the body as the need arises. One of its main disadvantages, however, is that it occupies one of the warrior's hands at all times, thus reducing his effectiveness as a fighter. This is why, in ancient times, a second person, called a "shield bearer," was often used to carry the warrior's shield for him.

The larger and heavier a shield is, the better protection it will provide, but a large and heavy shield requires more time and effort to carry about and move into position. Just as they were constantly seeking to strike the right balance between too much and too little armor, ancient armorers were also constantly trying to strike a balance between a shield that was too small and light and one that was too large and heavy.

A number of times in ancient history, the armies of one particular nation used exceptionally large shields with great effectiveness. In Mesopotamia, groups of soldiers equipped with large shields used the *phalanx* formation in their attacks. In this case, the mass of soldiers pressing close together created a solid wall of shields that was very effective against the spears and arrows of the enemy.

The Greek soldiers of the Bronze Age used a large shield made of thick animal hide stretched over a framework of wooden poles. This shield resembled a figure-eight in shape, and it curved around the warrior, protecting him from the sides as well as from the front. Finally, the Assyrian army of the years around 750 B.C. equipped some of their soldiers with large shields, but these shields were no burden at all to the soldiers they protected. Each soldier was also given his own personal shield bearer who followed the soldier around,

Soldiers of ancient Mesopotamia in the *phalanx* formation

holding the shield between him and his enemy.

Fairly small shields, both round and rectangular in shape, were also popular from time to time. The rectangular shield is the older type, but the round shield became the standard small shield of ancient times during the thousand years before the birth of Christ. The Greeks were especially fond of the round shield, which they began using during the Bronze Age. Later, when Greek civilization was enjoying its greatest power and prestige, the Greek soldiers used a round shield that was rather large as round shields go, about 40 inches (one meter) across. This famous shield was called the *hoplon* and the heavy infantrymen of Greece during this period were called *hoplites,* after the name of the shield they carried.

While other shields of that period had to be held with the hands, the inventive Greeks designed the *hoplon* so that the soldier could slip his left arm through a metal strap, thus supporting most of the weight of the shield on the arm, not the hand. The left hand grasped a leather strap near the edge of the shield to provide stability, but if the soldier needed to use his left hand in combat, he could do so without any risk of dropping the shield.

Shields were made of many different types of materials. You may be surprised to learn that while some ancient shields were made of metal, this was not always the best material for making shields. Leather shields were, in many cases, more effective than metal in providing protection from the blows of close-range weapons.

Right: An ancient helmet made of a natural mixture of gold and silver. (See the text on pp. 74-75.)

Overleaf left: The siege of an ancient city. The opposing armies battle with bows and arrows, while a battering ram hammers away at the city walls.

Overleaf right: This statue shows the Roman emperor Augustus dressed in molded plate armor.

Above: The picture on this vase shows a Greek warrior (left) armed with a spear and a *hoplon* shield confronting a Persian soldier who carries a composite bow and a *kopis* sword.

Left: A Greek *hoplite* and his arms are pictured on this pottery vessel from the sixth century B.C.

An interesting experiment was carried out at Oxford University in England to test the effectiveness of both leather and bronze as materials for making shields. The experimenters constructed two shields, exact duplicates of original museum pieces from ancient times. One was a bronze shield and the other was a shield made of leather; both were of similar size. The shields were tested against the blows of a large sabre and the jabs of a spear. The leather shield successfully withstood these blows and remained intact, but the bronze shield was both pierced by the spear and split by the sabre. Of course, the leather shield also had the advantage of being lighter than the bronze shield. As far as these two shields are concerned, there is little doubt that the leather shield was superior.

One of the best materials for shields was one of the cheapest and most plentiful materials available — wood. The *hoplon* was made of wood strengthened by a band of metal that circled the outer edge. The Romans used wood to make their most popular shield, and they also glued several layers of wood together to make a shield that we would call "laminated." This was actually an ancient form of plywood!

The wooden shields were often covered with leather for beauty and added strength. There were often metal ornaments on the front of a shield to serve as decorations and as a means of identifying the warrior who stood behind that shield. After all, the shields used by opposing armies might be nearly identical (it was not unusual, for example, for two Greek city-states to go to war against each other). It would be embarrassing, to say the least, if you were to attack a warrior and discover, after you had wounded him, that he was fighting on your side!

The Helmet

Since the head is probably the most vulnerable part of the human body, helmets have long been one of the most important pieces of defensive equipment. Unfortunately, few ancient helmets have survived, because they are made of thin sheets of metal that simply have not lasted intact after thousands of years in the soil. The metal helmets either rusted or corroded away, or were so crushed and mangled that it is impossible to reconstruct their original shape.

One of the few ancient helmets that did survive, however, was made of a natural mixture of gold and sil-

Soldiers of the Roman legions armed with shields, body armor, and helmets

ver, and for this reason it was not destroyed by time and the elements. It was undoubtedly a ceremonial helmet, because those soft metals would have provided almost no protection in battle. This helmet is made of a single piece of metal beaten into the desired shape. A row of small holes running completely around the edge of the helmet shows that it was once lined with a padding material that was sewn to the edge to protect the wearer from the sharpness of the bare metal.

While the inside of the helmet was made to fit the head of the wearer, the outside could be made in almost any shape. Some of the earliest helmets were metal caps with knobs, crests, horns, or cone-shaped projections that rose above the warrior's head. Many of these decorations were both large and impressive; they included crescents, horns, plumes of feathers or horsehair, and even the tails of certain animals.

The early helmets gave protection to the top of the head, but they left the ears and the back of the neck unprotected. From time to time, helmets were made with extensions that covered these areas, but most of the face still remained uncovered and open to attack. Then around 700 B.C., the Greeks developed a type of helmet that not only covered the top, back, and sides of the head but even curved around to the front of the head to protect most of the face, with only the eyes and mouth left exposed.

The main drawback of this type of helmet was that it interfered with both the hearing and the vision of the wearer. For the next 200 years, the Greeks experimented with many different types of helmets of this design, but they never found a way of completely eliminating its disadvantages. After 500 B.C., Greek soldiers returned to wearing the smaller, lighter, cheaper, and less protective helmet once again.

Body Armor

Making armor that protected the body was a far more difficult undertaking for the ancient armorer than making a helmet that protected the head. The problem is that in order to provide protection against weapons, the armor must be made of a material hard and stiff enough so that a blade could penetrate only with difficulty. At the same time, the armor had to be flexible, so that the wearer could move about freely.

One of the earliest forms of body armor was a heavy leather cape, often made with small metal rings

This ancient ruler wears a dome-shaped helmet equipped with metal flaps that cover his ears and neck.

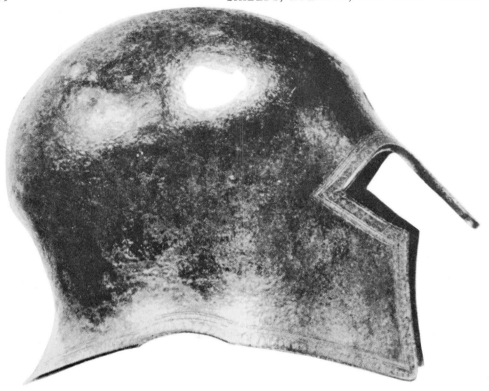

Above: A bronze helmet worn by Greek soldiers around 600 B.C. This helmet protected most of the face, leaving only the eyes and mouth exposed.

Left: A Greek warrior wearing a helmet made of the tusks of wild boars

sewn into its surface. Although this cape provided some protection, it could easily be penetrated by an arrow, a sword, or a spear. Some ancient people even used quilted cloth to protect the body. This material may have kept the soldiers warm in cold weather, but it offered little protection against the sharp points and blades of ancient weapons.

The best type of body armor was made of metal, although this material too presented problems to the ancient armorer. He had to make the armor heavy enough to repel weapons, yet light enough so as not to weigh the wearer down. At the same time, the suit of armor had to be flexible. Ancient people developed two different types of armor, rep-

Assyrian archers wearing long coats of scale armor

At first, the suits of scale armor, which were made in the shape of long cloaks, covered almost the entire body. As time passed, however, the coat was made shorter and shorter, until it had become only a tunic reaching to the knees.

The oldest example of armor from the West is some Greek armor made of bronze. It consists of two large plates shaped to fit the human body, one for the front and one for the back. Smaller strips of metal are joined to these two plates, to protect the neck, shoulders, and hips. In later periods, other versions of this type of armor were made by Greek and Roman armorers, who experimented with slightly different shapes and designs in an effort to produce a suit of armor that was both comfortable and protective. In the later days of

resenting two different ways of dealing with these problems.

In the East, armor was made of hundreds of small overlapping metal scales that were sewn onto a garment of leather or heavy cloth. While such armor was very flexible, it was also very heavy. Moreover, the many hundreds of scales that were needed for each suit of armor must have been expensive to produce and to sew onto the garment itself. For this reason, it is likely that only the commanders and most important warriors of the East wore armor in battle.

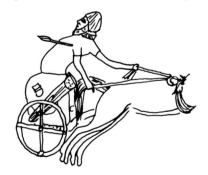

This detail of a drawing shows a Canaanite charioteer who has been hit between the scales of his armor.

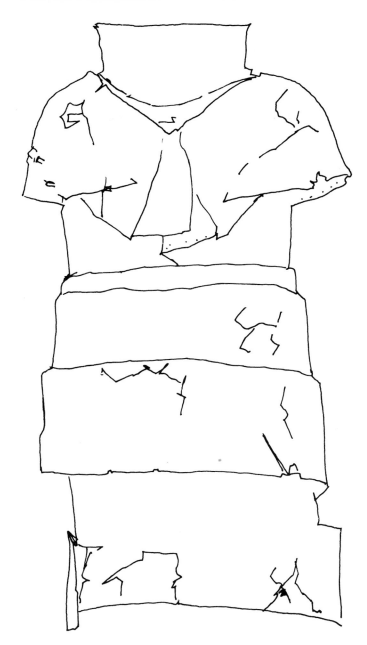

Bronze plate armor from Greece

A painting on a pottery vessel showing Greek warriors dressing for battle

This stone sculpture pictures Roman soldiers wearing segmented armor.

the Roman Empire, a type of plate armor made of a number of medium-sized segments was developed and made available to the professional Roman soldier. The individual pieces of this segmented armor were usually joined to each other by means of leather thongs. Sometimes, however, the pieces were sewn onto a separate leather garment.

An Assyrian cavalryman wearing a short coat of scale armor

When the warrior mounted on horseback became an important part of ancient warfare, the suit of armor took on new importance. First of all, the mounted soldier is an exposed target, and he therefore requires a kind of protection that covers his entire body while leaving his hands free. At the same time, the horseman does not have to carry the weight of armor on his own legs, so weight is not the kind of problem that it is for the foot soldier.

For these reasons, the horseman of ancient times gradually became heavily armored, and he began to assume a larger and larger share of the fighting. In late Roman times, the ordinary foot soldier, once the backbone of the Roman army, became less and less important. As time passed, his metal armor was taken away and replaced with leather armor. Then, even the leather garments were abandoned.

Meanwhile, the armor of the mounted soldier, or cavalryman, became more advanced, more complicated, and more expensive. Eventually, only the wealthy could afford to buy the armor needed to join the cavalry, and this part of the army became the special province of the upper class. Who would have guessed, when a Bronze-Age soldier buckled on the first suit of gleaming armor, that the equipment made to protect him from attack would eventually play a part in the division of Western society into an upper and a lower class?

VI THE FIRST ARTILLERY

Although there were no firearms in ancient times — no cannons, rockets, bombs, grenades, and guided missiles — there were still a few large and fearsome machines of destruction. These were designed for use not only against enemy troops but also against the defenses of fortified cities and towns.

The Catapult and Ballista

The catapult is a weapon designed to shoot heavy, arrow-like projectiles, and in many respects it is similar to a giant bow and arrow. Its power comes not from a wooden bow, however, but from fiber ropes that are twisted tightly and attached to wooden levers. When these levers are drawn back, they pull with tremendous force against a missile that is placed on a track or groove between them. When the levers are released, they snap forward, sending the missile hurtling down the track and into the air. Projectiles thrown in this manner could easily pierce the strongest armor, even at long distances.

The ballista was a machine designed to hurl huge stones. It operated in a manner similar to that of the catapult, except that the ballista had only one large lever with a pocket at the end into which the heavy stone was placed prior to firing. The lever was slowly cranked back into firing position, and, when the trigger was pulled, it snapped forward like a giant's arm, hurling the stone high into the air.

The full power of the catapult and ballista became evident during the siege of a fortified city, when the attacking army tried to break through the high stone walls of the fortifications. While soldiers were trying to dig under the walls or batter them down with a battering ram, the catapult and ballista were used to keep the city's defenders off the ramparts at the top. Otherwise, the rain of stones, arrows, boiling oil, and other dangerous and unpleasant objects

A ballista mounted on wheels, pictured in a carving on Trajan's Column in Rome

that they sent down from above would make it impossible for the attacking army to get close enough to the fortifications.

If the fortifications were particularly tall, the catapult and ballista would be placed on top of wooden towers — called "siege towers" — that were constructed on the spot by the attackers. These towers would give the catapults and ballistas even greater range, enabling them to fire their heavy stones and missiles deep inside the city walls.

One of the most gruesome yet imaginative uses of the ballista in ancient times was that made by a Roman general who showered pottery jars on his enemy's ships during a sea battle. The jars contained poisonous snakes, which were released, no doubt in an aroused and angry condition, when the jars smashed upon the ships' decks. This

A reconstruction of a Roman "onager," a machine used to hurl heavy stones

may be the first example of biological warfare on record!

The Battering Ram

The battering ram was the most effective weapon devised for breaking through the fortifications of a fortress or walled city. This machine was basically a long, heavy wooden shaft with a metal tip, and it was pounded against a spot in a stone wall until that spot weakened and became a hole. The hole was then enlarged until the attacking soldiers could pass through it into the interior of the city. In Roman times, the metal end of the shaft was made in the shape of a ram's head, and from this the battering ram got its name.

In the beginning, the long, heavy

The defenders of a besieged city throw down lighted torches in an attempt to set on fire a battering ram (left) that is about to break through the city walls.

beam of wood was held in the soldiers' hands and simply swung back and forth. But this enabled the defenders to fire at the attackers from above. Then the operation was improved by dragging a movable shed up to the walls of the city. The attackers could stand under the shed and swing the battering ram, more or less sheltered from the objects that were being thrown or fired at them. At some point, the heavy beam was simply hung from the roof of the shed by ropes. Then the soldiers could devote all their energies to swinging the ram and did not need to waste their strength merely holding it up off the ground. This method also made it easier to aim the head of the ram at exactly the same spot on the wall with each blow.

When the ancient fortresses and fortifications were constructed, the builders usually tried to incorporate some kind of defense against the battering ram into their design. The best defense was to surround the walls themselves with steep slopes. If the slopes were steep enough, the heavy battering ram could not be wheeled close enough to the wall to reach it. In such cases, there was only one way in which the attackers could reach the wall with their battering ram, and that was by building a ramp that began some distance away from the fortress and went up at a gradual slope, ending in a level area next to the wall. Building such a ramp was a slow, difficult, and dangerous task, but it was often the only way of getting the ram up to the wall.

When the ramp was completed and the battering ram moved into position, the defenders' only hope was to try to put the ram out of commission. They might throw stones and other heavy objects down in an effort to break the shaft of the ram, but the strong, armored roof of the protective shed usually made this impossible. Another method was to set the ram on fire by pouring buckets of oil on the leather-covered roof of the shed and then throwing down lighted torches. This method of defense was so common, in fact, that the sheds of some ancient battering rams were built to hold tanks of water for fighting these fires. Other methods of defense were also used from time to time. In at least one case, the defenders of a city tried to snare the ram with chains, and in another case, the defenders lowered a huge pad of straw into place in front of the ram to soften its blows.

While such methods certainly created difficulties for the attackers, they rarely accomplished more than just postponing the inevitable. In the end, the battering ram usually succeeded in breaching the wall, and once the attacking forces made their way inside the fortifications, the inhabitants were usually quickly defeated. The battering ram was probably the most successful of all the large war machines built in ancient times. Not until the development of firearms and cannons was it replaced by weapons of greater usefulness in siege warfare.

Weapons in ancient times were made and used quite differently from the weapons we are familiar with today. In many ways, our tanks, planes, explosives, and firearms are more destructive than the weapons of the past. The ancient warrior, for all his skill and courage, would be no match for a modern combat soldier armed with the latest automatic weapons. Our modern weapons are more deadly, because they can effortlessly shatter the human body in an instant. On the other hand, the ancient weapons were perhaps more cruel, because the warrior using them was often staring into the face of his opponent as he injured or even killed him. This probably required a degree of heartlessness not demanded of a soldier who is aiming only at a series of blips on a radar screen.

Today, the weapons of ancient times are curiosities, kept in museums for the human race to learn from and wonder about. Perhaps, with luck, human beings will eventually learn to live without violence and war, and *all* weapons will become museum pieces, the objects of curiosity, wonder — and horror — to the people of future generations.

GLOSSARY

archer	A soldier who specialized in the use of the bow and arrow
ballista	A war machine designed to hurl heavy objects, such as stones, over great distances
bronze	A mixture of copper and tin, widely used in ancient times for making tools and weapons
catapult	A war machine designed to shoot heavy missiles at high speed
chariot	A small, open wagon used in warfare, designed to be pulled at high speed by horses
composite bow	An advanced type of bow, made of several different materials glued together
gladius	The principal sword of the Roman soldier
hafting	The process of attaching the point or blade of a tool or weapon to its handle
hoplon	A large round shield, used by the infantry in Classical Greece
javelin	A lance or spear designed especially to be thrown as a medium-range missile

mace	A war club to which a heavy weight of stone or metal has been attached
phalanx	A tight formation of spearmen, used during attacks
quiver	A cylindrical container for storing and carrying arrows and javelins
rapier	A long, straight sword with a thin blade, used for thrusting
reinforced bow	A wooden bow reinforced with an elastic material such as sinew to prevent it from snapping when bent
sabre	A broad, heavy sword, used for striking and slashing
sickle-sword	An ancient weapon with a curved blade and a long handle, used as a sabre
simple bow	A wooden bow made of one solid piece, lacking reinforcement
sling	A device used for hurling stones
slinger	A soldier who specialized in the use of the sling in warfare
socket	A tube-shaped addition to a point or blade, used for hafting
tang	A projecting tongue of metal, used for hafting a point or blade

INDEX

Pages listed in italic contain illustrations only.

ACKNOWLEDGMENTS

The illustrations are reproduced through the courtesy of: British Museum P. 8; 10; 16; 18; 45; 54; 57; 67; 88. Archaeological Receipts Fund, Ministry of Science, Greece P. 11; 46; 53; 78. Metropolitan Museum of Art, Fletcher Fund P. 13; Rogers Fund P. 61; 73. Alinari P. 14; 38; 39; 48−49; 75; 86; 87. Israel Department of Antiquities and Museums P. 15; 77. Israel Museum, Photo David Harris P. 24. Cairo Museum P. 25; 27; 29; 31; 32; 78. Massada Press P. 33−36; 68−71. A.C.L., Bruxelles P. 40. Chuseville, Paris P. 43. Hirmer Fotoarchiv, Munich P. 47. Baghdad Museum P. 58. Louvre Museum, Paris P. 60; 64; 84. Ashmolean Museum P. 62. Drawings by Ofra Kamar P. 26; 81. Deutsches Archäologisches Institut, Athens P. 79. Kunsthistorisches Museum, Wien P. 82.